The Tithing Hoax:

Exposing the Lies, Misinterpretations & False Teachings about Tithing

R. Renee   *   Cynthia Harper

A Publication of Ross~Michel Publishing

The Tithing Hoax: Exposing the Lies, Misinterpretations & False Teachings about Tithing

Copyright © 2008 by R. Renee & Cynthia Harper

ISBN 978-1-105-42801-2

The Tithing Hoax is a publication of Ross~Michel Publishing.

Scripture quotations are taken from the Holy Bible, King James Version

Acknowledgements

We give all praises to our Creator. We thank everyone for reading our book. We hope you receive it in the Spirit in which it is written.

Peace & Blessings,

R. Renee

Cynthia Harper

The Tithing Hoax

Table of Contents

Part One
The Gospel of Greed

Part Two
The Truth about Tithing

Part Three
The Rest of the Truth – Q & A

Preface

The practice of tithing is a long held tradition in the Christian church. It is also a sensitive topic that stirs a great deal of controversy and debate. Many argue that the Bible commands Christians to tithe. Yet we contend that tithing is an obsolete practice that is not applicable to Christians. So who's right? Should Christians tithe?

The Tithing Hoax answers these and other questions. It uncovers the truth about tithing that may anger some and enlighten others. A book of this nature will challenge many Christians to rethink their traditional beliefs about tithing. Ultimately, *The Tithing Hoax* aims to *expose* and *correct* the false doctrines that keep Christians in religious and financial bondage.

Introduction

It is important that Christians read, study and research the Bible. If not, Christians run the risk of being exploited and led astray by false teachings. Most Christians assume that everything they hear from preachers is biblically correct. However, this is not always the case.

For example, we were taught that money is the root of all evil. We were led to believe that money is evil and poverty is righteous. This formed the basis of a "pie-in-the-sky" doctrine that promised Christians a reward after they had died and gone to heaven.

We now know this doctrine or belief system was based on a misquotation of biblical scripture. The Bible says, "The _love_ of money is the root of all evil." In other words, greed is the root of all evil—not money. Therefore, the proper reading and understanding of that verse has helped change the negative attitude towards money. The church, by and large, no longer views money as evil. However, the changing attitude toward money has resulted in another "pie-in-the-sky" type doctrine called the "Prosperity Gospel."

Many preachers who teach this doctrine assert that Christians must tithe in order to receive God's financial blessings. However, a careful study of the scriptures actually disputes this popular doctrine.

In 1 Thessalonians 5:21 it says, *"Prove all things; hold fast that which is good."* The Bible encourages us to question what we hear and read. As it relates to tithing and prosperity, we must ask the following questions: *What is a tithe? What was the purpose of the tithe? Who does the Bible say should tithe? Who should receive tithes? Did early Christians tithe? Is tithing applicable to today's Christians? Does the Bible teach that tithing leads to financial blessings?* If we want to answer these questions, we must place the practice of tithing within its proper biblical context.

There are two forms of context that we must consider: *literary* and *historical*. Literary context answers the questions of *who, what, when, where, how* and *why* as it relates to a particular biblical verse or scripture. In understanding a verse or scripture we must read the passages before and after a verse. In other words read the whole chapter. This allows us to understand a given verse in its proper context. However, literary context alone is not enough for us to have a true understanding of the scriptures.

We must also read the Bible within its historical context. Historical context takes into account the language, culture, customs, political and social climate of the ancient world. The Bible was not written in a vacuum. The biblical authors were influenced by their environment. So once we understand the literary and historical context of the scriptures then we can determine its application.

There are three categories of application: *specific, universal* and *selective*. Specific application means the scripture *only* applies to the individual or people who are addressed in the text. For example, the Mosaic Law was given *specifically* to ancient Israel. Therefore, the Mosaic Law applies to the ancient Israelites. Universal application refers to scriptures that are relevant to all believers. These scriptures are general in nature and speak to the human condition. The Book of Proverbs is a prime example of scriptures that have universal application.

In the selective application process some Christian preachers select scriptures relating to ancient biblical practices and customs and apply them to modern Christianity without any regard to the contemporary relevance of these ancient practices and customs. They also select and apply biblical scriptures according to how they fit into a particular doctrine. For example, the Prosperity Gospel is based in part on scriptures taken out of context and scriptural misinterpretations, especially as it relates to tithing. Selective application, as practiced in this manner, is deceptive because it uses the Bible to support ill-conceived beliefs, teachings and doctrines.

False teachings and doctrines regarding tithing flourish in the body of Christ because many Christians do not question what is taught. No man-made doctrine can serve as a substitute for truth. It is not enough to know what the Bible *says;* we must also know what the Bible *means* by what it says. If we desire truth, we must be followers of Christ—not followers of men.

Part One
The Gospel of Greed

Isaiah 56:11

"Yea, *they* are greedy dogs *which* can never have enough, and they *are* shepherds *that* cannot understand: they all look to their own way, every one for his gain, from his quarter."

Chapter 1

Prosperity Gospel:
A Christian Lottery?

 he Prosperity Gospel is a popular but controversial doctrine. Many Prosperity Gospel preachers proclaim that diligent "tithing" and unyielding faith are essential in receiving God's blessings. They place strong emphasis on paying so-called tithes as the key to unlocking the door to financial wealth, health

and prosperity.

If you want a new car, you must pay tithes. If you want a new home, you must pay tithes. If you want to live debt-free, you must pay tithes. People love the idea of obtaining riches. Therefore, the Prosperity Gospel and similar doctrines have become very popular among many Christians.

Some critics call the Prosperity Gospel the "Christian lottery." They say the doctrine treats God (or church/ministry) like a lottery machine. The tithe is the token. As with gambling, if you put enough tokens (tithes) into the lottery machine (church/ministry), hopefully you will win (receive blessings). Unfortunately, many Christians find themselves disillusioned. Despite paying so-called tithes, they are not receiving "miraculous" financial blessings or breakthroughs. Thus, the biblical and spiritual accuracy of the Prosperity Gospel comes into question.

Is the Prosperity Gospel a false doctrine?

The Prosperity Gospel, as it is taught, is not biblically accurate. First, the Bible does not say Christians will receive health, wealth and prosperity in exchange for paying so-called tithes. Secondly, the biblical tithe did not consist of giving money. Thirdly, the Bible does not command Christians to tithe. In fact the Bible makes no mention of Christians ever paying tithes. Yet despite what the Bible actually says about tithing many preachers still preach this false gospel.

There is nothing wrong with preaching prosperity. Nevertheless, we believe the Prosperity Gospel gives Christians a distorted view of God and prosperity.

Many preachers are preaching prosperity in a manner that is not consistent with the Bible. We believe the Prosperity Gospel is based on scriptural misinterpretations and/or greed. Scriptures related to tithing are often taken out of context. This creates a false doctrine(s). Many Prosperity Gospel preachers then present this false doctrine(s) to Christians as the "word of God." And now millions of Christians are caught up in a false doctrine(s) that exploits them financially and weakens them spiritually.

Chapter 2

Rich Preachers, Poor Christians

 hy do some preachers teach false doctrines about tithing? One answer: It generates millions of dollars.

"Get-rich-quick" minded preachers understand that so-called tithing is essential in making them rich. They stress that Christians should pay so-called tithes in order to receive blessings and riches. Thus, the Prosperity Gospel and similar doctrines financially benefit many preachers.

Many preachers live opulent lifestyles. Some preachers become very wealthy. Some live in expensive homes. Some wear expensive tailored suits. Some drive luxury cars. In addition, we see more and more extravagant church buildings.   We are witnessing the exponential growth in congregations across the nation.   Some of this growth can be attributed to the allure of the Prosperity Gospel doctrine.   But at what cost is the Christian church experiencing this growth?

Millions of Christians fall under the spell of "tithing equals blessings." The vast majority of Christians are the poor and working class. Many of them are in debt. Many are in desperate situations so anything that sounds good or promises a better life will appeal to them. So they give their hard earned money (so-called tithes) in hopes of obtaining financial prosperity.   In the meantime, these preachers are collecting so-called tithes and *their* bank accounts are growing while their congregants continue to struggle.

Moreover, the Prosperity Gospel and similar doctrines emphasize the pursuit of material possessions. This is materialism – not biblical prosperity. The Bible speaks to the corruptible influence of materialism.

Lest when thou hast eaten and art full, and hast built goodly houses, and dwelt therein; And when thy herds and thy flocks multiply, and thy silver and thy gold is multiplied, and all that thou hast is multiplied; Then thine heart be lifted up, and thou forget, the LORD thy God, which brought thee forth out of the land of Egypt, from the house of bondage (Deuteronomy 8:12-14).

In this instance, Israel was chastised because they forgot about God when their wealth increased.

The Bible gives another example of how spiritual poverty can exist in the midst of financial prosperity. The Bible illustrates this point, when it compares the poverty stricken church in Smyrna to the wealthy church in Laodicea.

I know thy works [referring to the church in Smyrna], *and tribulation, and poverty, (but thou art rich)...* (Revelation 2:9).

The church in Smyrna was materially poor but *spiritually rich*.

Because thou [referring to the church in Laodecia] *sayest, I am rich, and increased with goods, and have need of nothing; and knowest not that thou art wretched, and miserable, and poor, and blind, and naked* (Revelations 3:17).

The church in Laodicea was very wealthy. They made the mistake of equating financial prosperity with spiritual well-being. As a result, they were blind or unaware of their spiritual shortcomings. The Bible teaches us that financial prosperity is not always an indication of *spiritual wealth* or *maturity*.

We live in a materialistic society in which money is god and greed is the religion. The Prosperity Gospel's focus on money, wealth and riches places the Christian church in the same state as the church of Laodicea. Like the Laodiceans, today's Christian church does not see that it is spiritually poor.

The Bible does not condemn wealth, but it does teach that spiritual well-being is more important than obtaining material possessions. The Bible teaches that man can not serve both God and mammon (i.e. money). The greed and materialism in the church have blurred the line between God and mammon. Thus, it is not always clear as to whether some preachers are serving God or mammon.

A preacher's wealth is not always evidence of God's blessings. In many cases, the preacher's financial prosperity is evidence of his/her ability to manipulate and exploit their congregants. These preachers are prosperous because they have convinced millions of Christians that God commands them to pay so-called tithes.

There is no arguing that there is a need for money to operate a church and/or ministry. However, the misuse of the Bible to make some preachers rich at the expense of the masses is unacceptable.

Chapter 3

Keeping It Real about Prosperity

any Christians who go to church and pay so-called tithes on a regular basis never obtain wealth or prosperity. One reason for this is the lack of proper spiritual guidance and financial instruction.

Many preachers offer Christians religious rituals and false

doctrines in the place of truth, wisdom and spiritual principles.

The key to true prosperity is very simple. It involves discovering your God-given talent(s), and using that talent(s) to serve the needs of humanity. You possess skills, talents and gifts that are unique to you. No one else in the world can express those skills, talents and gifts the way you do, and therein lies your purpose. And where your purpose is there also is your provision and prosperity.

Biblical prosperity does not require the payment of so-called tithes. Satisfying fleshly desires is not the purpose of biblical prosperity. Biblical prosperity is the means by which God blesses you in order for you to be a blessing to others.

A sound ministry or church empowers people to help themselves. It empowers those who are marginalized in our society. It offers *practical* solutions to everyday problems. For example, a ministry that is devoted to prospering its members will offer classes and/or workshops on real estate investments, entrepreneurship, debt management, credit repair, etc. These are ministries of self-empowerment and self-improvement.

Our advice is to be mindful of preachers, ministries and doctrines that offer false hope and "pie-in-the-sky" promises. Be mindful of preachers who only entertain you. Be mindful of preachers who play on your emotions from Sunday to Sunday and pacify you for a moment. Be mindful of those who still preach so-called tithing as a means of becoming prosperous. Furthermore, read the Bible for yourself and *"study to show thyself approved."*

Chapter 4

Tithing, Faith & Foolishness

here is a huge difference between being faithful and being foolish. For example, you have $600 to pay your rent. This is all the money you have. Your preacher says "pay your tithes." So you take $60 and pay the so-called tithe. Now you are $60 short on your rent and facing possible eviction.

This Christian is now depending on God to miraculously send the $60 they need for their rent.

Is this faith or foolishness?

In this case, this Christian is being foolish. This Christian fails to realize God blessed them with the $600 to pay their rent. Instead, the Christian took their rent money and paid the so-called tithes to the preacher/church. Not only is this foolish but it is also poor financial stewardship.

The Bible promotes good financial stewardship. Your first financial obligation is to take care of your household expenses. Like Jesus said, *"Render therefore unto Caesar the things which are Caesar's."* The money that you have to pay for your household expenses does not belong to you, God, the preacher or the church. It belongs to the utilities company, the mortgage company, the landlord, etc. Good financial stewardship starts with taking care of your responsibilities first and foremost.

Faith is good. However, misdirected faith leads to foolish behavior and unnecessary stress.

Bible promotes good financial stewardship.

Take care of your financial responsibilities

Chapter 5

Tithers vs. Non-Tithers

ome preachers create a "tithers" vs. "non-tithers" atmosphere in their church. While watching television, I witnessed a preacher telling his congregation that if they did not tithe, God would not bless them. He went on to say that those who did not tithe blocked the blessings of those who did tithe. He was placing pressure on the church members who did not tithe or could not afford to tithe. Furthermore, he was coercing Christians into paying so-called tithes by employing blame, guilt and embarrassment.

In some churches "non-tithers" are treated like second-class Christians. Some churches refuse to help those in need because they do not tithe. I saw one Prosperity Gospel preacher on television who openly admitted that he refused to lay hands on a church member who did not tithe. He went on to boast that he turned away another non-tither who needed assistance with paying bills. In my opinion, this gave the impression that Christians who did not pay so-called tithes were not worthy or deserving of God's blessings – or his church's assistance.

Can you imagine Jesus refusing to heal the sick because they had not paid tithes? Imagine Jesus checking the church records to see if Lazarus paid tithes before raising him from the dead? We know Jesus did not practice his ministry in this fashion. We know Jesus did not require payment or a tithe for his teachings and healings. Jesus' ministry was based on a love for humanity. He did not discriminate between those who paid tithes and those who did not.

Chapter 6

Exposing the Tithing Hoax

any preachers either intentionally or unintentionally misrepresent the true meaning and practice of biblical tithing. The most common teachings about tithing do not line up with biblical scriptures. In response to these false teachings, we conducted our own study and research.

Studying or researching the topic of tithing does not require one to have attended seminary. One does not need a Ph.D. in theology. One does not have to be a bishop, preacher, pastor or teacher to understand the meaning of biblical tithing. Frankly, all one needs is to be able to read and understand biblical scriptures within a literary and historical context.

We read and studied the Bible, and we find that the Bible is very clear as to the meaning and purpose of tithing. The following chapters represent our findings which expose and debunk the false teachings surrounding tithing. According to the Bible, Christians are not obligated or commanded to tithe. Tithing, as it is commonly taught and practiced today, has no place in the Christian church.

Part Two
The Truth about Tithing

Ephesians 4:14-15

That we *henceforth* be no more children, tossed to and fro, and carried about with every wind of doctrine, by the sleight of men, *and* cunning craftiness whereby they lie and wait to deceive; but speaking the truth in love, may grow up into him in all things, which is the head, *even* Christ.

Chapter 7

Christians Were Not Commanded to Tithe

 ccording to scripture, the only people in the Bible commanded to tithe were the ancient Israelites (Hebrews/Jews). Tithing was part of the Mosaic Law of the Old Testament. Biblical tithing was an elaborate system of ceremonial rituals involving animal sacrifices. Biblical tithing was practiced as a

means of cleansing Israel of sin, but it also served other purposes.

Firstly, Israel's tithing was a means of honoring God. Israel was given a decree to keep God first in their lives. They gave a tithe (tenth) of their agricultural produce and offered it to God. Tithing from the land was an ongoing reminder that God was the source of their blessings. It served as a constant reminder to keep God first.

And thou shalt eat before the Lord thy God, in the place which he shall choose to place his name there, the tithe of thy corn, of thy wine, and of thine oil, and the firstlings of thy herds and of thy flocks; **that thou mayest learn to fear the Lord thy God always** *(Deuteronomy 14:23).*

Secondly, according to biblical scripture, God commanded Israel to give tithes to the Levitical priests. God chose the Levites to serve as priests and rulers for the nation of Israel. They were responsible for conducting Israel's religious worship and ceremonial rituals.

The tribe of Levi was the only tribe that did not receive a land inheritance. Without land they had no means of supporting themselves. Thus, the other eleven tribes gave a tithe (tenth) of all their land produce to the tribe of Levi.

At that time the LORD separated the tribe of Levi, to bear the ark of the covenant of the LORD, to stand before the LORD to minister unto him, and to bless in his name, unto this day. Wherefore, **Levi hath no part nor inheritance with his brethren**; *the LORD is his inheritance, according as the LORD thy God promised him (Deuteronomy 10:8-9).*

Take heed to thyself that thou forsake not the Levite as long as thou livest upon the earth (Deuteronomy 12:19).

*And the Levite that is within thy gates; **thou shalt not forsake him: for he hath no part, nor inheritance with thee*** (Deuteronomy 14:27).

For the LORD thy God has chosen him out, of all thy tribes, to stand to minister in the name of the LORD, him and his sons for ever (Deuteronomy 18:5).

Lastly, the Mosaic Law also included the giving of tithes to the widows, fatherless and the strangers within the nation of Israel. Israel was commanded to tithe as a means of taking care of the less fortunate. Tithing was a social support system for those without land or family. In this regard tithing instilled the importance and necessity of communal cooperation.

*And the Levite, (because he hath no part nor inheritance with thee,) and **the stranger, and the fatherless, and the widow**, which are within thy gates, shall come, and shall eat and be satisfied; that the LORD thy God may bless thee in all the work of thine hand which thou doest* (Deuteronomy 14:29).

*Then thou shalt say before the LORD thy God, I have brought away the hallowed things out of mine house, and also have given them unto the Levite, and unto the **stranger, to the fatherless, and to the widow**, according to all thy commandments, which thou hast commanded me: I have not transgressed thy commandments, neither have I forgotten them* (Deuteronomy 26:13).

The biblical tithe served both the religious and practical needs of Israel. Tithing was a means by which Israel honored God. Under the Mosaic Law the tithe was collected from the eleven tribes of Israel and given to the Levites. Finally, it was a form of communal support for those in need. Above all, biblical tithing is a commandment of the Mosaic Law given *only* to ancient Israel.

Chapter 8

Tithing Did Not Consist of Money

T he Mosaic Law commanded Israel to tithe. A tithe literally means a tenth or ten percent. Since Israel was commanded to pay ten percent, we must ask ten percent of what?

The ancient Hebrews lived in a predominately agricultural-based society. Therefore their tithe consisted of fruits, vegetables, grains, oils, animals, wine, etc. In turn, this produce was sacrificed and offered unto the Lord.

And all the tithe of the land, whether of the seed of the land, or the fruit of the tree, is the LORD's: it is holy unto the LORD (Leviticus 27:30).

Thou shalt truly tithe all the increase of thy seed, that the field bringeth forth year by year (Deuteronomy 14:22).

And concerning the children of Israel and Judah, that dwelt in the cities of Judah, they also brought in the tithe of oxen and sheep, and the tithe of holy things which were consecrated unto the Lord their God, and laid them by heaps (2 Chronicles 31:6).

Although the ancient Hebrews lived in a predominately agricultural-based economy, a monetary system did exist during that time. The Bible gives numerous examples in which silver and gold were used as a means of currency and exchange.

My lord, hearken unto me; the land is worth four hundred shekels of silver; what is that betwixt me and thee? Bury therefore thy dead. And Abraham hearkened unto Eprhon; and Abraham weighted to Ephron the silver, which he had named in the audience of the sons of Heth, four hundred shekels of silver, current money with the merchant. In this example, Abraham purchased a field with silver measured in shekels (100 shekels) to buy his wife Sarah a burial place. In addition, Jacob purchased land with pieces of silver (Genesis 23: 15-16).

And he bought a parcel of a field, *where he had spread his tent, at the hand of the children of Hamor, Shechem's father,* **for an hundred pieces of money** (Genesis 33:19).

Despite the availability of money (silver and gold), biblical scripture makes it clear that God did not command the payment of tithes in the form of money. In other words, the biblical tithe did not consist of money. However, the Bible makes reference that the Israelites could redeem (exchange) money for their tithe (food/drink).

Prior to the building of the Jewish Temples, ancient Israel did not have a centralized location to take their tithe (food/drink). They had to transport their tithe to a designated location. For some the distance was too far to transport their tithe (food/drink). Their tithe (food/drink) would have spoiled or perished by the time they arrived at the designated location. Therefore, special arrangements were made for the Israelites in this situation.

Once they arrived at the location, the money was exchanged (redeemed) for the tithe (food/drink).

And if the way be too long for thee, so that thou are not able to carry it; or if the place be too far from thee, which the LORD thy God shall choose to set his name there, when the LORD thy God hath blessed thee: then shalt thou turn it into money, and bind up the money in thine hand, and shalt go unto the place which the LORD thy God shall choose: And thy shalt bestow that money for whatsoever thy so lusteth after, for oxen, or for sheep, or for wine, or for strong drink, or for whatsoever thy soul desire: And thy shalt eat there before the LORD thy God, and thou shalt rejoice, thou, and thine household (Deuteronomy 14:24-26).

Some preachers today argue that food was used for tithes because money was not available during biblical times. This is why some preachers attempt to justify paying tithes in the form of money today. But as we see from biblical scripture, money was readily available. However, money was not acceptable for the purpose of tithing.

Therefore, there is no biblical basis for paying a monetary tithe.

Chapter 9

Tithing Places Christians Under a Curse

he Mosaic Law was given to ancient Israel. The Mosaic Law is *one* Law consisting of *hundreds* of commandments. The tithe command is only *one* of many commandments. According to biblical scripture, ancient Israel was cursed if *all* of the commandments were not followed.

*But it shall come to pass, if thou will not hearken unto the voice of the LORD thy God, to **observe to do all his commandments** and his statutes which I command thee this day; that all these curses shall come up on thee, and overtake thee* (Deuteronomy 28:15).

According to verses 16-68, the curses included disease, war, drought, plagues, oppression, poverty, drought, military defeat, captivity by the enemy, etc.

For the sake of argument let's say Christians are commanded to tithe. If this were so, Christians would be under the Mosaic Law because tithing is a Mosaic Law practice. Thus, there are two reasons why we believe tithing is a curse for Christians.

First, a Christian who tithes but does not follow the other commandments is breaking the Law. According to biblical scripture, anyone following the Mosaic Law must follow *all* of the commandments. Thus, they are cursed.

*For as many as are of the works of the law are under the curse: for it is written, **Cursed is every one that continueth not in all things which are written in the book of the law** to do them* (Galatians 3:10).

For whosoever shall keep the whole law, and yet offend in one point, he is guilty of all (James 2:10).

Second, the biblical tithe did not consist of money. Biblical scripture states that tithes consisted of agricultural products such as fruits, vegetables, grains, oil, spice, and cattle. Many Christians consider biblical tithing as giving ten percent of one's income to a church, ministry or preacher. Christians who tithe in the form of money are breaking the Law. Therefore, they are cursed. The Mosaic

Law was *one* Law that required strict observance of *all* commandments. The tithe command was not viewed as being separate and apart from the rest of the Mosaic Law.

Chapter 10

Tithing is a Rejection of Jesus the Christ

iblical tithing was a system of religious rituals consisting of animal sacrifices and offerings. The blood of the animal was intended to cleanse ancient Israel of sin. However, scripture states such sacrifices were not sufficient for the cleansing of sin.

For it is not possible that the blood of bulls and of goats should take away sins (Hebrews 10:4).

In the Old Testament a male lamb was sacrificed. The blood of the lamb was offered up unto the Lord for the remission of sins. As stated above animal sacrifices were not suitable for the cleansing of sin. Thus, Jesus became the only sacrificial "lamb of God" that was suitable for sacrifice.

The next day John seeth Jesus coming unto him, and saith, Behold the Lamb of God, which taketh away the sin of the world (John 1:29).

The Mosaic Law foreshadowed the coming of the Messiah.

For the law having a shadow of good things to come, and not the very image of the things, can never with those sacrifices which they offered year by year continually make the comers thereunto perfect (Hebrews 10:1).

According to scripture, Jesus was the Messiah who would cleanse humankind of sin. Moreover, the death, burial and resurrection of Jesus the Christ fulfilled the Mosaic Law, which includes tithing.

Think not that I am come to destroy the law, or the prophets: I am not come to destroy, but to fulfil (Matthew 5:17).

And he said unto them, These are the words which I spake unto you, while I was yet with you, that all things must be fulfilled, which are written in the

Law of Moses, and in the prophets, and in the psalms, concerning me (Luke 24:44).

For Christ is the end of the law for righteousness to every one that believeth (Romans 10:4).

Christ has redeemed us from the curse of the law, being made a curse for us: for it is written, Cursed is everyone that hangeth on a tree (Galatians 3:13).

In other words, the death, burial and resurrection of Jesus the Christ replaced the need for the Mosaic Law, including tithing (i.e. animal sacrifices). "*Now where remission of these is, there is no more offering for sin* (Hebrews 10:18)." Thus, the Mosaic Law is obsolete. Since tithing is part of the Mosaic Law it too is obsolete and not a part of New Testament Christianity.

Wherefore the law was our schoolmaster to bring us unto Christ, that we might be justified by faith. But after that faith is come, we are no longer under a schoolmaster (Galatians 3:24-25).

In that he saith, a new covenant, he hath made the first old. Now that which decayeth and waxeth old is ready to vanish away (Hebrews 8:13).

The death, burial and resurrection of Jesus the Christ ushered in a new covenant (i.e., New Testament). The following scriptures serve as reminders that Christians are not obligated to follow the Mosaic Law, which includes the practice of tithing. In addition, these scriptures emphasize the importance of living according to the *spiritual principles* taught in the New Testament.

*Who also hath made us able **ministers of the new testament**; not of the letter, but of the spirit: **for the letter killeth**, but the spirit giveth life* (2 Corinthians 3:6).

*But now **we are delivered from the law**, that being dead wherein we were held; that we should **serve in newness of spirit**, and **not in the oldness of the letter*** (Romans 7:6).

*For **Christ is the end of the law** for righteousness to every one that believeth* (Romans 10:4).

For I through the law am dead to the law, that I might live unto God (Galatians 2:19).

*I do not frustrate the grace of God: **for if righteousness come by the law, then Christ is dead in vain*** (Galatians 2:21).

*O foolish Galatians, who hath bewitched you, that ye should not obey the truth, before whose eyes Jesus Christ hath been evidently set forth, crucified among you? **This only would I learn of you, Received ye the Spirit by the works of the law, or by the hearing of faith?** Are ye so foolish? Having begun in the Spirit, are ye now made perfect by the flesh? Have ye suffered so many things in vain? If it be yet in vain. **He therefore that ministereth to you the Spirit, and worketh miracles among you, doeth he it by the works of the law, or by the hearing of faith*** (Galatians 3: 1-5)?

But before faith came, we were kept under the law, shut up unto the faith which should afterwards be revealed (Galatians 3: 23).

For ye are all the children of God by faith in Christ Jesus (Galatians 3: 26).

The primary purpose of the biblical tithe was to cleanse ancient Israel of its sin. Nevertheless, the blood of animals was not sufficient for the cleansing of sin. According to scripture, Jesus was the Messiah foreshadowed in the Old Testament and the only perfect "lamb" that could save humankind and cleanse the world of sin. *But with the precious blood of Christ, as of a lamb without blemish and without spot* (1 Peter 1:19). Therefore, Christians are saved by the blood of Jesus. Thus, when Christians pay so-called tithes, they are in fact rejecting the death, burial and resurrection of their savior.

For the law was given by Moses, but grace and truth come by Jesus Christ (John 1:17).

Chapter 11

New Testament Christians
Did Not Tithe

C hristianity derived from Jewish religious traditions, rituals and ceremonies. In fact, the first Christians were Jewish. However, there were several aspects of Judaism that were not incorporated into Christianity.

For example, some Jewish Christians believed Gentiles (non-Jewish people) should be circumcised in order to convert to Christianity. They also wanted the Gentiles to follow the Mosaic Law. However, the Apostle Paul and others disagreed. They did not believe circumcision or the observance of the Mosaic Law were necessary for a Gentile to become a Christian (Acts 15). Therefore, circumcision did not become a part of Christianity. Like circumcision, tithing was another Jewish ritual that was not carried over into Christianity.

There are a number of New Testament scriptures that make reference to the fact that the death, burial and resurrection of Jesus the Christ brought an end to the Mosaic Law, which includes tithing.

Having abolished in his flesh the enmity, even the law of commandments contained in ordinances; for to make in himself of twain one new man, so making peace (Ephesians 2:15).

Blotting out the handwriting of ordinances that was against us, which was contrary to us, and took it out of the way, nailing it to his cross. (Colossians 2:14).

For there is verily a disannulling of the commandment going before for the weakness and unprofitableness thereof (Hebrews 7:18).

In that he saith, A new covenant, he hath made the first old. Now that which decayeth and waxeth old is ready to vanish away (Hebrews 8:13).

According to biblical scripture, Jewish Christians and Gentile Christians believed Jesus the Christ was the Messiah. Moreover, they believed the death, burial and resurrection of Jesus the Christ fulfilled the Mosaic Law. What this means is that there was no longer a need, reason or purpose for biblical tithing (animal sacrifices).

This is why the New Testament makes no mention of Christians tithing.

Chapter 12

Giving Replaced Tithing

ithing and giving are two entirely different biblical practices. The difference is not merely a matter of semantics. They are different concepts, and it is incorrect to use the words interchangeably. Biblical tithing is a Mosaic Law commandment given to ancient Israel whereas giving is a *spiritual principle* practiced among New Testament Christians.

*Every man according as he purposeth, in his heart, so let him **give**; not grudgingly, or of necessity: for God loveth a cheerful **giver** (2* Corinthians 9:7).

Notice the verse does not say let him "tithe" nor does it say a cheerful "tither."

The apostles practiced the act of ***giving***. When they fellowshipped, they broke bread with one another and prayed. They also provided for one another's needs. According to biblical scripture, the apostles sold possessions and goods and distributed the proceeds for the benefit of those in need (*Acts 2: 42-47*).

Giving, unlike biblical tithing, is a *voluntary* act. Nowhere in the New Testament are Christians *commanded* to give. Giving is *encouraged* but never commanded. Furthermore, the scriptures make it clear that giving should not be a burden to the giver. The Bible teaches us that giving is neither an obligation nor should it be a hardship.

*Now therefore perform the doing of it; that as there was a readiness to will, so there may be a performance also out of that which ye hath. For if there be first a willing mind, it is accepted according to that a man hath, and not according to that he hath not. **For I mean not that other men be eased, and ye be burdened**: but by equality, that now at this time **your abundance** may be a supply for their want, that **their abundance** also may be a supply for your want: that there may be equality* (2 Corinthians 8:11-14).

The Bible encourages one to give according to one's ability. In other words we should give according to what we can *afford*.

*Then, the disciples, every man **according to his ability**, determined to send
relief unto the brethren which dwelt in Judaea (Acts 11:29).*

The Bible does not promote poor financial stewardship. We
believe an individual should take care of their personal
responsibilities and financial obligations *before* they give. That which
is left is your abundance, and it is out of your abundance that you
give.

Moreover, unlike biblical tithing, there are no restrictions with
giving. In addition, giving is not limited to money. Christians can
give less than or more than ten percent of *anything* they have. One
can give money, food, time, talents, etc. The only condition, if you
will, is that one gives out of a love for God and others. Therefore,
one's attitude or motivation for giving is just as important, if not more
important, than the act of giving itself.

The death, burial and resurrection of Jesus the Christ ushered in
the New Testament. Under the New Testament giving replaced
tithing. According to biblical scripture, tithing is an obsolete religious
practice that passed away with the Mosaic Law. However, giving is
an eternal spiritual principle based on love and an intimate
relationship with God.

Part Three
The Rest of the Truth – Q & A

John 8:32

"And ye shall know the truth, and the truth shall make you free."

Abraham, Jacob & Pre-law Tithing

What is "pre-law tithing"?

The first reference to the tithe is in the book of Genesis in which Abram presents King/Priest Melchizedek with a tithe (tenth) of the spoils he obtained in battle. This act of tithing took place hundreds of years before the establishment of The Mosaic Law. Hence, the phrase "pre-law tithing."

Did Abram establish a "tithe law"?

No. There is a false teaching within the body of Christ that says Abram established a so-called tithe law. Some preachers assume that Abram's tithe to King/Priest Melchizedek is evidence that

God established a "tithe law" prior to the Mosaic Law. However, this is not true.

A law is like a commandment. It is something that must be done. Therefore, if tithing was God's "law" the scriptures would note that God commanded or spoke to Abram to tithe. Yet, nowhere in the scriptures does it say God commanded Abram to give a tithe to King/Priest Melchizedek. Whenever God commanded Abram (Abraham) to do something, the Bible says: "God commanded" or "God spoke" to Abram (Abraham). "The Lord had said unto Abram…" (Genesis 12:1) or "And the Lord appeared unto Abram, and said…" (Genesis 12:7). According to biblical scripture, God commands Abram (Abraham) to perform several acts. For example, God commanded him to leave his people, sacrifice his son Isaac, circumcise his sons, etc.

Finally, Abram's tithe to King/Priest Melchizedek was strictly voluntary. Abram gave a tithe to the King/Priest Melchizedek because it was part of the ancient social custom of his day.

Did Jacob tithe because of a "tithe law"?

The next time tithing is mentioned in Genesis is in reference to Jacob – Abraham's grandson.

*And Jacob vowed a vow, saying, **If** God will be with me, and will keep me in this way that I go, and will give me bread to eat, and raiment to put on, So that I come again to my father's house in peace; **then** shall the LORD be my God: And this stone, which I have set for a pillar, shall be God's house: and of all that thou shalt give me I will surely give the tenth unto thee* (Genesis 28:20-22).

Jacob's tithe was voluntary and conditional. Jacob promises to give

God a tithe *if* God blesses him. In other words, Jacob wanted blessings from God *before* he gave a tithe. If there was a "tithe law" in place, Jacob would not have approached God in this manner. If a "tithe law" existed, as some preachers teach, Jacob would have said: "**I will give God a tenth whether God blesses me or not**." Yet Jacob is negotiating or bargaining with God.

If a "tithe law" existed, Jacob would have given a tenth of whatever he had without any negotiation. Instead he makes a conditional vow of paying tithes *only* if God blesses him. The fact that Jacob's tithe was voluntary and conditional is further evidence that a "tithe law" did not exist.

Why do some preachers teach that tithing is a "law" Christians must follow?

We believe some preachers teach the "tithe law" because they do not know any better. While some know better, they refuse to teach the truth for a number of reasons (e.g., financial gain).

Many preachers know that tithing is an obsolete religious ritual that is not part of New Testament Christianity. Therefore, they need a way of justifying Christians paying so-called tithes (money). We believe this is why the false doctrine of Abram's "tithe law" is taught today.

Some preachers argue that this so-called "tithe law" is part of the New Testament. They attempt to use Abram's tithe as "evidence" that God had a "tithe law" in place hundreds of years before the Mosaic Law. According to these preachers, the so-called tithe law did not pass away with the Mosaic Law. They suggest the so-called tithe law was carried over into the New Testament. Therefore, Christians are required to pay tithes (money).

Of course, this is not true. Nothing in the Old Testament or the New Testament supports this foolish doctrine. Nowhere in the Bible are Christians ever commanded to tithe in any form or fashion.

Why did Abram give King/Priest Melchizedek a tithe?

Abram's tithe was a *voluntary* act of gratitude for his successful win in battle (Genesis 14:11-24).

Since Abram/Abraham is considered the "father" of Christianity, shouldn't Christians tithe because Abram/Abraham tithed?

Abraham, "the father of the faith", engaged in many pre-law practices that modern Christianity does not accept or practice. If a preacher says Christians should tithe because Abram tithed, then Christians should engage in every pre-law practice performed by Abram/Abraham. For example, Abram practiced polygamy (Genesis 16:1-2). Why embrace tithing and reject polygamy. Why isn't polygamy, like tithing, considered a "law" of God carried over into the New Testament and applicable to Christians?

There is a distinction between a social custom/practice and a spiritual/universal law. The tithe, as mentioned in Genesis, was a social custom/practice. Many preachers who proclaim Christians should tithe because Abram tithed are driven by ignorance, greed and/or self-gain.

Did Abram's tithe make him wealthy?

No. Preachers who tell their congregation that tithing made Abram wealthy are in error.

Abram was a wealthy man *before* he gave a tithe (tenth) of the war spoils to King/Priest Melchizedek. There is no link between his tithe and his wealth. He did not tithe in order to obtain wealth. And he was exceedingly wealthy before he gave a tithe to King/Priest Melchizedek (*Genesis 13:2*).

Genesis 13:2

"And Abram was very rich in cattle, in silver, and in gold."

Furthermore, King/Priest Melchizedek offers Abram the goods from the war. However, Abram declines King/Priest Melchizedek's offer. He says, *That I will not take from a thread even to a shoelatchet, and that I will not take any thing that is thine, lest thou shouldest say, I have made Abram rich* (Genesis 14:23).

If Abram's tithe did not make him wealthy, how did he acquire his riches?

The Bible tells us exactly how Abram became an exceedingly wealthy man, and it has nothing to do with tithing. By most accounts, Abram was a farmer by vocation. He acquired his wealth by way of his vocation as a farmer. He later increased his wealth when Pharaoh gave him riches in exchange for his wife Sarai.

Genesis 12:10-20 tells the story of how Abram and his wife Sarai traveled into Egypt to escape a famine. Abram asked Sarai to say she was his sister. Apparently in ancient times a husband traveling with his wife was likely to be killed if someone wanted the husband's wife. We can infer that a brother travelling with his sister would be safe from harm. Thus, Abram was protecting himself from any potential harm while he and Sarai journeyed to Egypt.

The scriptures tell us Sarai was very beautiful. She was so beautiful that once in Egypt, Pharaoh took notice of her and made her his wife. Pharaoh thought Sarai and Abram were sister and brother. In exchange for Sarai Pharaoh gave Abram sheep, oxen, donkeys, slaves and camels. In other words, Abram received riches in exchange for his wife. Eventually Pharaoh found out Sarai was Abram's wife. In fear of being cursed Pharaoh banished Abram and Sarai from Egypt. However, when they left, they left with the riches Pharaoh gave Abram.

Thus, the Bible makes it clear Abram's wealth was not the result of so-called tithing.

The Levitical Priests & Tithes

Who were the Levitical priests?

The Levitical priests were the religious rulers of Israel. They offered tithes to the Lord on behalf of Israel. The tithes were sacrificial offerings given for the cleansing of Israel's sins.

All the priests of Israel were selected from the tribe of Levi; hence the name Levitical priests. All the priests were Levites; however, not all Levites were priests.

The only Levites selected for the priesthood were those who were descendents of Moses' brother Aaron.

And take thou unto thee Aaron thy brother, and his sons with him, from among the children of Israel, that he may minister unto me in the priest's office, even Aaron, Nadab and Abihu, Eleazar and thamar, Aaron's sons (Exodus 28:1).

The other Levites assisted the priests in performing functions within the Jewish Tabernacle and Temple.

Why did the Levitical priests receive tithes?

They were the only tribe that did not receive a land inheritance. They were not given land to farm because they had to devote all their time to conducting religious ceremonies and to performing civic functions for Israel. Thus, the other eleven tribes were commanded to give the Levites tithes in order to support them.

Wherefore Levi hath no part nor inheritance with his brethren; the LORD is his inheritance, according as the Lord thy God promised him (Deuteronomy 10:9).

Are today's preachers the same, equivalent or continuation of the Levitical priesthood?

No. Levitical priesthood and Christian preachers are similar in that they perform religious services. However, the similarity ends there.

Firstly, the Levitical priesthood was based on heredity. The priests were chosen from the tribe of Levi. Aaron and his descendents were chosen as high priests. In fact, Israel was cursed when they appointed priests who were not in the lineage of

Aaron (*1 Kings 13:33-34*). Christian preachers are not descendents of the tribe of Levi and Aaron.

Secondly, Levitical priests bore the sins of the nation of Israel.

And the Lord said unto Aaron, Thou and thy sons and thy father's house with thee shall bear the iniquity of the sanctuary (Numbers 18:1).

But the Levites shall do the service of the tabernacle of the congregation, and they shall bear their iniquity (Numbers 18:23).

The Levitical priests were responsible for cleansing Israel of sin. Christian preachers do not bear the sins of Christian believers.

Thirdly, the Levitical priesthood was replaced with the priesthood of Christ (Hebrews 5 & 7). According to scripture, all Christian believers are priests.

But ye are a chosen generation, a royal priesthood (I Peter 2:9).

And hath made us unto our God kings and priests (Revelation 5:10).

Many Christians are taught that preachers are the same as Levitical priests. Based on this teaching, they believe preachers are justified in receiving tithes. However, we see that this is a false teaching. Levitical priests and Christian preachers are not the same. Moreover, the Bible does not command payment of tithes to Christian preachers.

Malachi & Tithes

What did Malachi mean when he said, "Will a man rob God"?

The book of Malachi is frequently quoted for the purpose of justifying and promoting tithing. A Christian is accused of robbing God when he or she does not pay so-called tithes. It is also used to condemn Christians who do not tithe. We believe some preachers use Malachi to bully their congregations into tithing. However, a closer reading of Malachi indicates that the prophet Malachi is criticizing Israel's *religious leaders* (i.e., Levitical priests) who did not tithe according to the Mosaic Law.

According to Malachi, the Levitical priests were robbing God. They robbed God by not tithing. They also robbed God when they gave blemished offerings that were not suitable for sacrifice (*Malachi*

1: 7; 3: 8-10). The priests were responsible for bringing acceptable tithes to the altar. The tithe was offered to cleanse Israel of sin. However, when the priests did not tithe according to the Mosaic Law, they placed themselves and Israel under a curse.

*And now, O ye **priests, this commandment is for you**. If ye will not hear, and if ye will not lay it to heart, to give glory unto my name, saith the LORD of hosts, I will even send a curse upon you, and **I will curse your blessings**: yea, I have cursed them already, because ye do not lay it to heart* (Malachi 2: 1-2).

Israel relied on the Levitical priests for all of its religious guidance and instruction. Israel did not perceive of a one-on-one relationship with God. The priests were intermediaries between Israel and God. When the priests failed to fulfill their obligations to God and the people, the prophet Malachi rebukes the priests.

The book of Malachi addresses an issue much deeper than tithing. Malachi is pointing out how corrupt religious leadership causes people to stray from God. The book of Malachi is a message and a warning to false prophets and deceptive religious leaders. Malachi says, **"For the priests lips should keep knowledge, and they should seek the law at his mouth: for he is the messenger of the LORD of hosts** (*Malachi 2: 7-8*). In other words, the most important thing for religious leaders to do is to speak truth to the people.

Unfortunately, many of today's preachers are not proclaiming the truth about tithes. It is erroneous for any preacher to use the book of Malachi to condemn Christians who do not pay so-called tithes. It is also inappropriate to coerce Christian into paying so-called tithes.

What is a blemished offering?

According to scripture, a blemished offering consisted of animals that were sick, diseased, lame, etc. (*Malachi 1:12-13*). Blemished offerings also included spoiled food, bruised fruits and vegetables, etc. A blemished tithe or offering was unacceptable for sacrifice.

Is it possible to rob God?

No. God is the Creator of all things. God is the Alpha and the Omega. There is nothing we can give to God that God does not already have. There is nothing we can take from God that God can not replenish.

Doesn't Malachi say God will bless Christians if they tithe?

No. The prophet Malachi is speaking to ancient Israel – not Christians. Malachi is reiterating a promise made to ancient Israel. The prophet is reminding ancient Israel that God would bless them as long as they followed *all* the commandments of the Mosaic Law.

The prophet Malachi writes that God will open up the windows of heaven and pour you out a blessing (*Malachi 3: 10*). In the book of Malachi, blessings from heaven are a reference to rain. Rain is the blessing because it was needed for the crops. Without rain, the crops would ruin and there would be no harvest.

Remember, ancient Israel lived in an agricultural-based economy, and they believed the giving of tithes (e.g., fruits, vegetables, and animals) would guarantee rain for their crops.

What does Malachi mean when he says, "Bring ye all the tithes into the storehouse?"

The exact quote is "Bring ye all the tithes into the storehouse, that there may be **meat** in mine house..." The reference to meat is found in *Malachi 3:10*. Here the tithe literally refers to meat. When the verse speaks of "meat," it means cattle and herds such as goats, lambs, cows, etc. It is not a reference to money. Malachi is not speaking of bringing money into a church.

Is the storehouse the same as a church?

The biblical storehouse is not a place of religious worship. A storehouse is not the same as a church. According to biblical scripture a storehouse is where crops, grains, wine and oils were stored.

And the famine was over all the face of the earth: and Joseph opened all the storehouses, and sold unto the Egyptians; and the famine waxed sore in the land of Egypt (Genesis 41:56).

And Hezekiah had exceedingly much riches and honour: and he made himself treasuries for silver, and for gold, and for precious stones, and for spices, and for shields, and for all manner of pleasant jewels; Storehouses also for the increase of corn, and wine, and oil; and stalls for all manner of beasts, and cotes for flocks (2 Chronicles 32:27-28).

Moreover, biblical tithes (i.e., food, grain, wine, oil, and cattle) were placed in storehouses until they were offered up as sacrifices. The translation of the word storehouse into the word church is erroneous. The biblical storehouse and the church are different entities and serve two entirely different purposes.

Should Christians tithe from their gross income?

The Bible does not address such an issue. What we do know is that the biblical tithe did not consist of money. The Bible does not teach that Christians should tithe from their gross or net income. We believe the notion of tithing from one's gross income is an example of a greed-driven, man-made, false doctrine.

First Fruits, Offerings & Tithes

Are first fruits the same as tithes?

No, they are not the same. First fruits refer to the first of the crops whereas tithes refer to a tenth of the crops. However, they do have some similarities. First, first fruits and tithes did not consist of money. Like tithes, first fruits were produce from the land. Second, first fruits and tithes were commandments given only to Israel. First fruit offerings, like tithing, are not part of New Testament Christianity.

That thou shalt take of the first fruit of all the fruit of the earth, which thou shalt bring of thy land that the LORD thy God giveth thee, and shalt put it in a basket, and shalt go unto the place which the LORD thy God shall to place his name there (Deuteronomy 26:2).

Are offerings the same as tithes?

No. <u>Biblical offerings were *voluntary* gifts</u>. Under the Mosaic Law biblical tithing was *mandatory* for ancient Israel.

*Take ye from among you an **offering** unto the LORD: **whosoever is of a willing heart**, let him bring it, an offering of the LORD* (Exodus 35:5).

*And they came, every one **whose heart stirred** him up, and **every one whom his spirit made willing**…And they came, both men and women, **as many as were willing hearted*** (Exodus 35:21-22).

*The children of Israel brought **a willing offering** unto the LORD, every man and woman, **whose heart made them willing** to bring for all manner of work, which the LORD had commanded to be made by the hand of Moses* (Exodus 35:29).

Is the widow's mite an example of tithing in the New Testament?

The widow's mite appears in the books of Mark 12:41-44 and Luke 21:4. The widow places two mites into the treasury. Some argue that the widow's mite is an example of tithing in the New Testament. They also suggest that the widow's mite is a *monetary* tithe. They are incorrect in both instances. According to scripture widows *received* tithes. Under the Mosaic Law, widows were not commanded to pay tithes. However, they were welcome to give free-will offerings. The widow was exempt from paying tithes. Thus, her mite was a voluntary, free-will offering.

The New Testament, Christians & Tithes

Did Jesus teach tithing?

Jesus was Jewish. He was not a Christian. Therefore, Jesus lived under the Mosaic Law. He was obligated to follow the commandments of the Mosaic Law. One of those commandments required tithing. Jesus was also a rabbi who taught according the Mosaic Law. Therefore, he taught tithing in addition to the other commandments.

Since Jesus mentions tithing in the New Testament, shouldn't Christians tithe?

In one instance, Jesus makes a reference to tithes in the Gospel of Matthew.

Woe unto you, scribes and Pharisees, hypocrites! for ye pay tithes of mint and anise and cummin, and have omitted the weightier matters of the law, judgment, mercy, and faith: these ought ye to have done, and not to leave the other undone (Matthew 23:23).

Jesus was speaking to the scribes and Pharisees who were also Jewish and followers of the Mosaic Law. Jesus scolds them for paying tithes while neglecting more important issues such as justice, mercy and faithfulness. As far as Jesus was concerned, the tithe was one of the least important commandments.

Furthermore, although Matthew and the other Gospels appear in the New Testament, the New Testament was not established until *after* the death, burial and resurrection of Jesus the Christ. It is at that time the New Testament replaced the Mosaic Law, which includes tithing. Therefore, when Jesus mentioned tithes he was referring to tithing as practiced under the Mosaic Law.

Should Christians pay tithes?

The Bible does not command or say Christians should tithe in any form. Tithing was a Jewish ceremonial ritual involving animal sacrifices. Tithing became obsolete along with the rest of the Mosaic Law. In other words, Mosaic Law tithing was replaced with New Testament giving.

Preachers, Prosperity & Tithes

Is the tithe a principle for prosperity?

No. Some preachers teach that the tithe or the practice of tithing is a spiritual principle for creating prosperity. Biblical tithing is a legalistic/religious practice. It is not a spiritual principle.

Jesus said, *"Seek ye first the kingdom of God and his righteousness and all these things will be added unto you."* This is an example of a spiritual principle. **Seeking God's kingdom** is the key to experiencing God's abundant blessings. Notice, Jesus did not say *tithe* and all these things will be added unto you.

I tithe, and I'm still broke. Why?

One reason is that the Bible does not promise Christians wealth and riches for paying so-called tithes. However, the main reason is poor financial stewardship.

Poor financial stewardship results from living beyond one's means. Many people want a "caviar lifestyle while living on a McDonald's budget." This is why Christians can pay so-called tithes and still struggle financially.

So-called tithing is not an answer to overcoming financial hardship. Overcoming financial hardships require *practical* solutions. Here are some examples:

The money used to pay so-called tithes can be used toward paying off a debt. If your expenses outweigh your income, then decrease your spending or increase your income. You can increase your income by acquiring more skills, training or education, getting a better job, budgeting your money, etc.

Once again, live within your means. Stick to a budget. Stop buying what you can not afford.

Will tithing make me wealthy or debt-free?

Absolutely not! Financial responsibility, saving money and making good investments create wealth. Living within your means will keep you debt-free – not so-called tithing. Nowhere in the Bible does it say that Christians are promised wealth if they tithe. Furthermore, Christians are not commanded to tithe, and tithing is not part of the Christian faith.

Isn't tithing part of good financial stewardship?

No. However, the Bible does promote good financial stewardship.

Good financial stewardship involves living within your means. Your first priority is to take care of your household necessities and responsibilities.

If tithing ended, why is it still taught in the church?

We believe the practice of so-called tithing continues because of biblical ignorance, religious tradition, fear and greed.

Many preachers do not know they are teaching a false doctrine. They have not taken the time to study and research tithing within its proper biblical context. Some preachers know better but they have not corrected their teachings. They do not want to stray from traditional doctrine – even if it is a false doctrine.

Some preachers fear that if they stop preaching so-called tithing their congregants will stop paying their money to the church/preacher. Many preachers depend on tithes to maintain an extravagant lifestyle. They believe if they stop preaching so-called tithing they will no longer be able to afford the lifestyle to which they have become accustomed.

If New Testament Christians did not tithe, how did tithing become part of Christianity?

Roman Emperor Charlemagne forced people to pay tithes. Charlemagne made tithing a civil law at the end of the eighth century (*Catholic Encyclopedia 1913*).

Is there a role for money in the church?

Absolutely. However, we believe there is not a role for so-called tithing. Biblical tithing and giving are not the same. With that said, there is a role for *giving* money to support one's church.

It takes money to effectively run a church or ministry. For example, church's need funds to operate outreach and community programs. Church's also have expenses such as water, gas, electricity, mortgage, etc.

Moreover, we believe the church functions as an organization. Like most organizations members give to support the function and activities of the organization. However, we do not agree with the tactics and false teachings on tithing many preachers use to coerce or manipulate their congregants, which is most often for self-gain.

Remember your giving is not limited to money. You can give of your time, talents, gifts, skills, expertise, etc. Give out of your love for God. Give what you can, when you can. Do not give out of fear that you will not be blessed.

NOTES

NOTES

NOTES

NOTES

NOTES

NOTES

A Message from the Authors

Beloved, we pray that this book has been a blessing to you and has opened your mind and Spirit to the truth regarding tithing. Thank you for taking the time to read this book. May the Creator bless you in all areas of your life.

Proverbs 4:7

"Wisdom is the principle thing; therefore get wisdom: and with all thy getting get understanding."

About the Authors

R. Renee is a poet, author, and teacher. Cynthia Harper is a speaker, teacher, and author. They also host a popular internet talk show called *The Naked Truth*.

Made in the USA
San Bernardino, CA
30 December 2017